Reflections Of A Man II
THE JOURNEY BEGINS WITH YOU

ROAM II

MR. AMARI SOUL

Reflections Of A Man II

THE JOURNEY BEGINS WITH YOU

Black Castle Media Group, Inc.

Black Castle Media Group books may be purchased for educational, business, or sales promotional use. For information, please email contact@blackcastlemediagroup.com

www.blackcastlemediagroup.com

First Edition

Cover Design by: BCMG

Cover Photography by: Brandon Harris

Library of Congress Cataloging-in-Publication Data has been applied for.

Paperback Edition	978-0-9861647-7-4
Kindle Edition	978-0-9861647-9-8
EPUB Edition	978-0-9861647-8-1
Hardback Edition	978-1-7338546-9-6

This book is dedicated to you,
the Beautiful, Strong Woman.

CONTENTS

INTRODUCTION   1

CHAPTERS
PART I - FOR YOU

TRAPPED   9
THE DECISION   19
NO MORE OF YOUR SPACE   29
LETTING GO OF THE PAIN   43
GETTING PAST THE DOUBT & THE GUILT   53
NEVER SAY BROKEN   63
THE FEAR OF A NEW LOVE   71
BREATHE   81
YOU ARE STILL BEAUTIFUL...
YOU ARE STILL STRONG   87
THE GOOD WOMAN   101
KNOWING THE DIFFERENCE   109
REMEMBER THIS...   115

CHAPTERS

PART II - FOR HIM

A TIME TO REFLECT   131
A NEW LEVEL OF UNDERSTANDING   139
EXPRESS YOURSELF   151

PART III - FOR BOTH OF YOU

MAKING IT WORK II   161
INTIMATE MOMENTS   171

PART IV - MY FINAL CHAPTER

NAKED   181
ACKNOWLEDGMENTS   195

www.mramarisoul.com
www.facebook.com/mr.amarisoul
www.instagram.com/mr.amarisoul
www.twitter.com/mramarisoul
www.pinterest.com/mramarisoul

Introduction

If the Wrong Man was honest,
this is what he would say to you...

My Intentions?

What are my intentions?
I mean, we are cool and everything,
but I'm not trying to be with you forever.
To me, this whole thing is temporary
but I won't say that.
You say you want to know my intentions... really?
I don't think you do because if you really knew,
it would make you sick to your stomach to know
that I don't really care about you.
I care that you let me drive your car.
I care that you give me half of your check;
I care that we have amazing sex and that's all cool,
but to be honest,
if all that stopped today...
I would leave you and be on to someone new.

I'll Manipulate You With Compliments

*I only pay you compliments to get you
to lower your guard;
I need time...
time to fill your head with all the things
you want to hear.
I'll never love you, but I'll act like I do
just long enough to get everything I want from you.
Deep down inside you know I'm wrong for you,
but my words and my act are so strong
that you ignore your intuition even when I slip up.
Now, I've got you right where I need you to be...
ignoring what you know is best for you
and already making excuses for me.*

My Hidden Motive

The reason why I talk down to you and consistently
belittle you is because I am emotionally insecure
and spiritually broken.
I know you deserve better and I'm afraid that one day
you'll realize this and leave me.
I'll never meet your standards, so I'll continue to
beat you down mentally and emotionally in hopes that
I can break you down to my level.
Then, you'll begin to think you can do no better.
Even when I treat you so wrong that you finally
get up the courage to leave,
your new insecurities will always lead you
right back to me.

What...

You Don't Trust Me?

Every time you get close to catching me,
I use my favorite mind game line on you:
"What... you don't trust me?
You want to look at my phone... for what?
You're invading my privacy,"
or at least that's what I want you to think.
You see, it's not about my personal space or privacy,
it's about all these pictures and phone numbers I've
been collecting for a while, and I know that if you were
ever to figure out my password, it would be over.
So, I hit you with the old , "What... You don't trust me?"
Then, I get mad and start pointing the finger at you
to get the focus off of me and to put it all on you.
So just know that every time you get close, I'm going to
say, "What... You don't trust me?"
That should put you back in your place.

The Truth Is...

I'm broken, and you can't fix me.
It doesn't matter how hard you try...
It doesn't matter how many changes you make
to yourself to appease me.
In the end, I'll still be broken,
and if you're not careful...

I'LL BREAK YOU TOO!

Do I have your attention now?

Part 1
For You

CHAPTER

One

TRAPPED

I hear your cries...
From behind his invisible walls of silence,
I hear your cries.
I close my eyes and I see through yours,
and as we stare at the world from behind closed doors...
I hear your cries.

Lost In The Wrong Man's Shadow

"When you have been in a relationship for so long and have played the supportive role to the Wrong Man's dreams and ambitions at the very expense of your own, you begin to feel as if you can't survive without him.... like without him, you're nothing."

The Wrong Man in your life knows these feelings all too well. Why? Because often times it's his words and or his actions that act as the planters of the seeds. As the seeds of doubt begin to grow, you start to question your own purpose in life and wonder whether or not you even have the ability to make it on your own. You often find yourself asking, "What if I leave? Where will I go? What will I do? What if he's right and without him I really am nothing...What if?"

My dear Beautiful, Strong Woman... Breathe. Though it may seem like you are trapped, with nowhere to turn, you always have options. They may not be easy but, nevertheless, you still have the power to break free of his hold. Dig deep down into the very depths of who you are and find that strength which rests within you. Where there is a will, there is always a way. It's never too late.

His Emotional Punching Bag

"Being strong does not mean you have to continue to put up with the Wrong Man's disrespect and abuse day after day and night after night. Who says that a Good Woman's role is to be the emotional punching bag for the Wrong Man?"

Only the Wrong Man would see you in such a distorted way. For him to take out his emotional frustrations on you is not a sign of true love, it's a show of his lack of love and respect for you, as well as for himself.

My dear Beautiful, Strong Woman, if ever you feel like this is what your relationship has become, just know... this is not love; this is not your destiny. It doesn't matter what he says, this is not your role.

You Deserve Better

"Some of you feel hopeless...
like there is no way out of your current situation.
It's like the more you look for a way out,
the more hopeless it seems.
You've even had thoughts that maybe...
this is all you deserve."

This is the type of relationship that causes you to break down and cry in the middle of the day or night for what seems like no reason at all. It's the type of relationship where his words and his actions have caused you to feel so insecure about yourself that you begin to doubt your own self-worth. You find yourself walking past the mirror with your head down... too afraid to look up out of fear of what you might see.

My dear Beautiful, Strong Woman, never second-guess your worth. The issue is not that you deserve less, the issue is that you have been willing to settle for less than what you deserve. This means, if you want things to change, you have to start with you. No longer can it be okay for you to accept less than what you need both spiritually and emotionally, as a Good Woman, in your relationship. No more excuses for him! No longer will you lower your standards just because it's the easy thing to do or because you are afraid of the possibility of being alone! Remember, being alone won't break your heart, feeling lonely in a relationship and settling for a man who doesn't value you will.

The Question You've Been Afraid To Ask

*Why do you hold on so tight to someone who would
let you go in the blink of an eye...
someone who doesn't even respect you enough to
come home to you at night... Why?
Are you afraid of being alone...
not realizing that right now, each night you are alone in
your own home because that man is
all wrong for you...
Why?
Is it the ticking of the clock?
Are you afraid that this may be your last chance at love
before the ticking stops?
My dear Beautiful, Strong Woman...
Let go of your fears and stop counting the years
because God is timeless. And since God is love,
just know it's not the years,
but your own fears that confine you.*

"Him" Then Vs. "Him" Now

*It's not always the reality of who he "IS" now
that keeps you holding on.
Sometimes, it's all the memories of who he "WAS" or
who he "CLAIMED TO BE" in the beginning
and your hope that one day that man will reappear
and somehow change things back to the way
they used to be...
That's what keeps you.*

Trapped In Your Own Mind

"Sometimes, it's not him... it's you."

Sometimes, it's the Wrong Man and his manipulations that cause you to feel trapped in an unhealthy relationship. Sometimes, it's his physical, mental and or emotional abuse. But other times, it's none of those things... it's you. It's you holding on so tight to the memories of the past that you begin to view things as they "were" and not as they "are." In your mind, you have, in a sense, trapped yourself in a relationship in which he has already let go of. All the pain you feel, the tightness in your chest, the anxiety that seems to take over out of nowhere... all of this because you are still holding on to something that no longer exists.

In this case, it's not him at all who's holding you prisoner... it's you.

Only You Possess The Key

"The key that sets you free is inside of you."

O nly you possess the key that truly sets you free. I won't tell you that it will be easy because it won't be. I won't tell you that the pain will all of a sudden disappear because it won't. I will tell you that nothing will change until you decide to change it; nothing will get better until you decide to stop accepting less than what you deserve. No one is going to come in and make that decision for you. The decision is yours to make and yours alone.

I pray that you find the strength and the courage to do what you know in your heart is best for your own happiness, sanity, and peace of mind.

CHAPTER

Two

THE
DECISION

You have to know what "You" want...
Do you want in, or do you want out?
Do you want to hold on, or do you want to let go?
What is it that you truly want?

The Battle Within

Why would you choose to stay?
Is it because your heart tells you it's the right thing to do
even when your mind knows that's just not true?
Why would you choose to stay when your heart aches
from all the pain?
Why would you choose to stay when you know
deep down inside he's the Wrong Man for you
and that things will never change... Why?
Is it love?
Is it hope?
Is it a combination of them both that causes you to
throw away all common sense and continue
to try to hold on to someone who has
already let you go... Why?

It's Never Really That Easy

Some people may say,
"You should just get over him and move on,"
as if it were that easy.
Maybe they don't understand what it's like to
give it everything you have...
to put your heart into someone and be forced
to make a decision:
"Do I leave or do I stay?"
Maybe they've never laid it all on the line because
if they had, they would know...
It's never really that easy.

Him Changing Won't Always Change Things

"When you have dealt with the nonsense for so long,
and the damage has already been done, the question is
no longer whether or not he'll change,
the question you now need to ask yourself is,
even if he did change... could you ever feel the same?"

Sometimes, things have gotten so bad that they're almost impossible to fix. You could ask him to change, and he could begin doing exactly what it is that you want him to do, but if too much damage has been done to the relationship, it will still feel wrong to you.

My thoughts... if he's hurt you really bad, to the point where you've begun to feel a deep resentment towards him, before you ask him to fix it, ask yourself this question: If he changed today and began doing everything right, would that change how you feel?

If it would, then maybe you could give it a try. If it wouldn't change the way you feel, let it go. Why? Because no matter what he does, no matter how hard he tries, it will never be enough for you. The damage has already been done.

The Fear
Of
Being Alone

"Some of you are holding on, not because it's worth holding on to, but because you're afraid of what will happen if you let go."

For some of you, it's not the love that you are holding on to, it's the fear... the fear of you being alone and not being able to find someone else if you decide to leave. It's all the "what if" questions that play over and over in your head: "What if I make the wrong decision? What if he's about to change and all he needs is a little more time? What if what he says really is true... that no other man will ever want me? What will I do then? I'll have nothing."

My dear Beautiful, Strong Woman, fear is a strong force, but you are stronger. I know it can sometimes feel overwhelming but don't submit to it. If you decide to stay, let it be because you feel that is what's best for you. Don't stay simply because you're afraid of being alone.

If, on the other hand, you feel that staying will only make things worse and leaving truly is the best decision for you to make, you have to be strong enough to say, "No! I refuse to stay and allow my fears to sentence me to a lifetime of misery! Today... I do what's best for me!"

I Don't Blame You

I don't blame you for not wanting to walk away from
something you spent years of your life
trying to hold together.
I don't blame you for wanting to give it just one more
chance hoping this time everything will be different.
I don't blame you.
I don't blame you for wanting to fight every day to
save it. I don't blame you for wanting to be able to say
you did everything you could do until there was nothing
left for you to do but to walk away...
I don't blame you.

Walking away is never easy. Just know, once you've come to the realization that it's over and you've done everything in your power, to the point of exhaustion, to make it work and he still refuses to work with you, let it go. Why? Because the longer you wait, the harder it gets. The harder it gets, the more it hurts.

NOTES:

Below, I would like you to list the top five reasons why you feel staying with the Wrong Man is the best thing for you. Be honest with yourself about the current state of your relationship, how you feel emotionally and spiritually about it and the direction you feel it is now heading.

_____

_____

_____

_____

Now, I would like you to list the top five reasons why you feel letting go is the best thing for you. Remember, it's important for you to be honest. This is your book; these are your pages. Here lies your opportunity to lay it all out for only your eyes to see. Write down your thoughts and take an honest look at where you are.

_____

_____

_____

_____

_____

_____

And now...

Your decision: _____

CHAPTER

Three

NO MORE
OF
YOUR SPACE

As you walked out the door, the Wrong Man yelled,
"You'll never find another man who will
treat you the way I do!"
He didn't realize that was exactly what you were hoping...
to never meet another man who would
"Mistreat" you the way he did.

Breaking The Cycle

For so many years, nothing changed.
You brought it up over and over and still...
nothing changed.
Finally, you said, "ENOUGH" and walked away.

One month later he came back to you and said, "I've changed." You gave him a second chance, and now, several months into it, he's back to doing the same old thing. What do you do now? Do you stay and if so, for how long? One month? Two months? Five years? How long are you willing to keep the cycle going before you finally say, "NO MORE!"

My thoughts... there's nothing wrong with giving someone a second chance; however, if that second chance begins to look a lot like a second round of the same old thing... let it go. Why? Because the cycle will not stop on its own, you have to be the one to stop it.

Burning The Emotional Bridges

"Sometimes you have to burn those emotional bridges to protect yourself from the Wrong Man reaching out to you or you reaching back to him. When you do that, you leave yourself only one direction to move in... forward."

I f you hold on to the things that connect the two of you emotionally, you make it harder for yourself to move on. In your mind, there is always a little space that still belongs to him.

You have to remove that space and burn that bridge for good. If that means giving back the gifts he gave to you, then give them back. If it means not going to certain places that remind you of him, at least until you are fully over him, then stop going to those places. If it means changing your number or blocking his... whatever it takes to burn those bridges, do it. If you don't, the process becomes much longer and much harder.

Close The Door Behind You

Don't tolerate nonsense from an "Ex."
They're your "Ex" now...
Technically, all their rights and privileges to your time
and emotional space have been revoked!

If the Wrong Man calls you today, don't answer. If he stops by, don't open the door. If he sends you a message, don't read it, delete it. Please understand that he's not trying to make your day... he's trying to ruin it.

Nowhere is it written that you have to respond when he calls. Once you've determined that he's all wrong for you and you've made the decision to let it go, don't give him any more of your physical, mental or emotional space.

When you cut off his access, you reduce his ability to

get past your defenses. The more access you give to him, the greater his chances.

Remember, if you don't allow him the opportunity to get back into your space, he can't get inside your head. If he can't get back inside your head, he can never break your heart again.

Stop worrying about whether or not your "Ex"
is now happy in his new relationship.

Stop checking his Social Media accounts. Why? Because at this point, how he's doing shouldn't matter. What if he is happy? Does that change how he made you feel? Does it change the fact that you still feel the emotional scars of giving everything you had to a man who in the end, neglected you, disrespected you and cared little about your emotional well being? Does it? Or better yet, what if he is unhappy? Would that make you happy?

My thoughts... you'll never find true happiness for yourself looking for it in someone else's misery... let it go. If he's happy now, good for him. Now is your time to focus on "YOU" and what's truly best for "YOU."

But, I Really Do Miss Him

You say, "But, I really do miss him."
Hmm... do you?
What about him do you miss?
Is it all the promises he never kept?
Is it all the time he spent with you in the beginning but
stopped spending with you in the end?
Maybe it's the lies; maybe it's the cheating.
My dear Beautiful, Strong Woman...
What is it that you truly miss?
Is it the man "he is"
or is it the man "you wanted him to be?"

Loneliness Is Not A Reason

*"Some of you are considering going back to the Wrong
Man, not because he deserves a second chance,
but because loneliness has caused you to forget
why you left in the first place."*

Don't forget why you left. Don't forget how many chances were given. Don't forget how many promises were broken. Don't forget how you felt the moment you finally decided, "Enough!"

If loneliness has caused you to forget, let me remind you. You've come too far and worked too hard to remove yourself from a bad situation to let loneliness throw you right back into the fire!

Your "Ex" Could Ruin Everything

Your "Ex" could ruin any chances of you
moving forward if you let him.
He will smile and say all the things you want to hear,
but beware... it's not always love that brings him back.
Sometimes, he just doesn't want to see you happy
with someone else.

My thoughts... if you've finally gotten over the heartbreak and have found the strength and the courage to move on, think long and hard before you allow your "Ex" back into the picture. If you decide to let your guard down, you risk losing everything.

The Apology That May Never Come

"Some of you are still waiting...
waiting for the apology that may never come...
waiting for the moment when he finally realizes he lost
a good thing when he lost you. Some of you are still
waiting, but why... for closure?"

As long as you still care about what he says or what he thinks, you still care; you can't separate the two.

When you get to the point where you can make the decision to close that door with or without the apology, that's when you know you have truly moved on. Until then, he still has a hold on you.

The Chance
You May Never Get

Sometimes, it's not about what you needed to hear from
him. Sometimes, it's about what he
needed to hear from you.
All those years you tried to talk, but he would
cut you off and refused to listen.
All those years he finished your sentences for you and
tried to tell "You" how "You" felt instead of simply
allowing "You" to express yourself.
If only he knew just how simple the solution was
back then, maybe it could have been fixed.
Maybe there wouldn't have been that distance;
maybe there wouldn't have been so much pain,
so much frustration and resentment.
Maybe... just maybe things would have been so very
different if he would have just taken the time to listen.

S ome of you are at this point now... still hoping for the day when you finally get the chance to tell him exactly how you really feel... for you to be able to express to him all the things that you have kept bottled up inside because you weren't able to say them before. And now, when he calls, instead of ignoring the call, you pick it up hoping this is that moment.

My dear Beautiful, Strong Woman, you may never get that chance. The chance for you to express to him all the things that you have carried around in your heart all this time, that chance may never come. And you have to be okay with that. You have to be willing to accept it and move on. Is it frustrating? Yes, but just know the longer you carry those things around inside, the more opportunities you will give him to keep coming back into your life just to hurt you all over again. Today is the day you shut that door for good.

NOTES:

On the following pages, I want you to write down all the things you want to tell him. Cry if you need to... scream if you have to, but get it all out of your system right now. When you have finished, turn the page and let it go.

_____

_____

_____

_____

_____

_____

_____

_____

CHAPTER
Four
LETTING GO
OF
THE PAIN

Who Knows?

Who knows your pain?
Who knows what it feels like to put everything
you have into making it work
just to get nothing but lies in return?
Who knows what it feels like to get that knot
in the very pit of your stomach?
You know the knot that comes at that very moment
when you finally realize that
your worst fears have come true.
Tell me, who knows the true pain and the true
heartache of a Good Woman's past...
who knows but you.

You Can't Hold It In Forever

You can't hold it in forever.
That forced smile that looks so genuine until
the tears begin to follow,
the tightness in your throat
that makes it hard for you to swallow...
You can't hold it in forever.
All of your past disappointments, the heartbreaks, the
feeling that no matter how hard you try,
things will always end the same way...
You can't hold it in forever.
You wear the make-up as a disguise
and think that because it's waterproof no one
will ever notice that you've been crying.
You can't hold that pain in forever.
Sometimes, you just have to let it all out.

Conversations Of The Heart

You say, "I've lost a lot...
My heart is still broken, and I'm afraid.
I don't know if I could ever learn to love and trust again."

My dear Beautiful, Strong Woman, it's not about you "learning" to love and trust again, it's about whether or not you are willing to allow the Wrong Man of your past to prevent you from loving and trusting again. Don't continue to give him that power over you; you're in control.

Strength Vs. Courage

*"When it comes to pain, it's not about having
the strength to keep holding on to it;
it's about you having the courage to face it,
learn from it and to finally make the decision to let it go."*

Remember this: The pain was never meant for you to carry around in your heart forever. Holding on to it won't make you any stronger nor will ignoring it make it magically disappear. You have to make the decision to face it, acknowledge it, overcome it and finally let it go. Until you do that, you won't be able to truly move on.

Change Of Perspective

Let's look at this from a different perspective.
Maybe it's not so much the letting go part that hurts.
Maybe what hurts you the most is that
you are trying to hold on to someone who has
already decided to let you go... maybe that's it.
If you change your perspective, you may see
that it's the holding on that is causing you the pain,
not the letting go.
Truly letting go may be the one thing that finally
frees "You" from the pain.

Have You Ever Wondered...

Have you ever wondered what would happen if
you decided right now to let it go...
to let go of all the pent up frustration,
all the hurt, and all the pain?
What would happen if right now you decided,
"I'm done holding on to that which is weighing
so heavily on my soul?"
Just imagine what tomorrow would be like if
today you just decided...
to truly let it all go.

You Are The One You've Been Waiting For

There are no magical remedies nor is there a mystical person who is going to walk into your life and remove that pain for you...
You are who you've been waiting for.

Many of you have remained in the position of being hurt for so long because you are subconsciously waiting for some external force to come in and magically remove that pain from your heart. Some of you even believe that one day the Right Man for you will come into your life and take that pain away. The truth is, there will be no magical external force nor will there be a man who will come into your life and remove that pain for you. A Good Man may help to reduce the pain, but ultimately, if you don't face it, that pain will begin to weigh both of you down.

In the end, you'll end up single again, carrying the same pain and the only difference will be that you will now somewhat blame him too. Not because he caused the pain, but because in your mind you will hold him partially responsible for not being able to remove it.

My thoughts... the pain will not go anywhere until you decide to face it and go through the painful process of removing it. It's up to you now. Those around you can support you, we can cheer you on, but you have to be the one to connect to your spiritual essence and remove it. All the lies, all the abuses, all the negativity that has been planted... you have to be the one to pull them all up by their roots and replace the lies with the truth, the negativity with positive thoughts and the abuses with a newly healed perspective. You have to be willing to go through the process to get to the end; one day at a time... one step at a time. Then, you have to be willing to let it all go. If you don't, it will always be with you.

I say this only to say... Stop looking externally and start looking internally. The strength, the courage, the very thing that you have been waiting on for so long is already within you. My dear Beautiful, Strong Woman... You Are Who You've Been Waiting For.

CHAPTER

Five

GETTING PAST
THE DOUBT
& THE GUILT

"Stop beating yourself up over your past.
So the Wrong Man slipped through your defenses;
It's okay.
That doesn't make you any less of a woman.
It simply means that you have experienced life,
both the good and the bad, and you are still growing."

Sometimes,
You Just Can't Win

"When he's the Wrong Man,
he'll say you're complaining when you're simply
trying to communicate. When you stop trying to
communicate, he'll start complaining."

When he's all wrong, it doesn't matter what you do, he'll make it seem as if you're always at fault. It's a no win situation for you. If you try to communicate, he'll say you're "nagging." When you stop trying, he'll start complaining that you never talk to him so how is he supposed to know how you feel.

My thoughts... don't let his mind games cause you to feel as if you were wrong for trying to communicate how you felt.

In the end, no matter what you did, in his mind, you would have always been wrong.

Quality Time

You were never wrong for wanting to spend
"quality time" with your man.
You were not asking too much, and it doesn't mean
that you were "needy."
It simply means you understand the power of
"quality time." You understand that it may take only
"time" to help create the bond, but that it's going to take
"quality time" to solidify it and to help
the relationship grow.

One Size
Does Not Fit All

*"If you let the Wrong Man go and he turns out
to be the Right Man for the next woman he meets,
don't be upset.
Just because he was right for her
doesn't mean he would have ever been right for you."*

L adies... let's talk shoes! Let's say that you wear a
size 8. Now, someone surprises you with a pair
of the most beautiful shoes you've ever seen.
Everything is perfect except for one little detail... they're
a size 7. Now, you really like the shoes, so you decide to
wear them anyway. After a while, those shoes begin to
cause you so much pain that you can't bear it anymore

and you decide to return them.

While at the store, another woman walks in and grabs the very same pair of shoes. She tries them on, and they fit her perfectly. Why? Because her feet are a size 7. She then buys the shoes and walks out of the store happier than she's ever been before. Are you mad? Not at all because you know that those shoes would have never fit you. Even if she came right back into the store and tried to give the same pair of shoes back to you, you wouldn't take them. Why not? Because you remember all the pain those shoes caused you and you know that somewhere there's a size 8 waiting for you.

The moral of this story is... One size does not fit all. You can't force the Wrong Man into being the Right Man for you. It will never work. The pain you will cause yourself will be unbearable.

Do not feel guilty and do not begin to doubt yourself as if somehow you failed as a Good Woman, that's not it. In the end, you can't dwell on how the Wrong Man ultimately fits someone else; you have to stay focused on how the Right Man is supposed to fit you.

You Were Never Stupid

I have heard so many of you say you felt "stupid"
for staying and trying to make it work
even when deep down inside you knew
nothing would ever change.
My dear Beautiful Strong Woman...
you were never "stupid."
You were in love, and real love is not something
a Good Woman simply walks away from.
She fights for it! She cries for it!
She holds on to it until it burns
at the very core of her soul.
No... you were never "stupid." You were real.
If anyone was stupid, it was the Wrong Man
who lost you. Why?
Because he may never know just how close he came to
receiving the blessing of a lifetime.

You Are
Not Crazy

You're not crazy...
You're not crazy for wanting more from
a relationship than just a title.
You're not crazy for expecting to be treated with
the gentleness that God intended for you.
The Wrong Man told you that you were crazy because
he was too selfish, too inconsiderate,
or maybe he was just too afraid to admit that
he was the Wrong Man for you and
that you deserved better.
Whatever the case may be...
You're not crazy.

Some Men Just Don't Get It

Some men won't listen until
there's no one left to listen to,
they won't pay attention until
there's no one left to pay attention to...
they won't care until there's no one left to care for.

What do you do when you've given all that you have and you have nothing left to give... after you've tried and you've tried, and you've cried and you've cried, and that day finally comes when you realize this is not how you want to live your life? At that moment, should you feel guilty about walking away? Not at all. Why? Because in the end, you can't make it work alone; you need his help. You can love him, you can support him, you can do everything in your power to make it work, but if he's not willing to listen to you... if he's not willing to set aside his ego and work to better understand you, if that man is not willing to stand up and fight side by side with you to save it, there's nothing else you can do except to walk away.

Just remember, when you finally do walk away, don't feel guilty and don't you dare allow him to make you feel as if only you are to blame... some men just don't get it.

Hold your head up and take comfort in knowing you did everything you could to hold on until there was nothing left to hold on to and your only option was to let go.

Rest Your Mind

Some men never grow up... They just grow older.

Remember, a man's maturity level and his readiness for commitment have less to do with his age and more to do with his mindset. Just because he's older, doesn't necessarily mean he's any more ready for a serious relationship today than he was 5-10 years ago.

CHAPTER

Six

NEVER SAY
BROKEN

The only person who can break you is YOU,
when you stop loving YOU.
As long as you don't stop loving yourself,
you can never be broken.

Blurred Vision

Some of you see yourself as being "broken."
You look at the scars left from the heartbreaks of
your past, and you believe you are not worthy of
self-love or the love of a Good Man.
You look down instead of up,
as if you have something to be ashamed of.

My dear Beautiful, Strong Woman, I'm not going to sit here and tell you to wipe the tears from your eyes because right now, I need you to cry like you have never cried before. I need you to get it all out of your system so that he can't hurt you anymore. But when you have finished, I need you to stand up and realize that you were never broken. You just needed a little more time, a little more space and a little more inspiration to move forward.

No More Of His Smoke & Mirrors

He may have broken your heart,
but he never broke you. He doesn't have that power.

W hat he did was distort your view. Think of it like a steamed mirror. When you stand in front of it, what do you see? You can't really see much, can you? But even still, you know you are standing there. Regardless as to what anyone says, you know that the distorted reflection you see is not a true representation of you and who you truly are. You understand that there is more to you than can be seen in the mirror at that moment.

Well, it's the same thing as when you believe you are broken. You've been standing in front of his clouded mirror for so long that he's convinced you that you are what he shows you.

My dear Beautiful, Strong Woman, remove that which clouds your view, and you'll see that Beautiful, Strong Woman is still standing there right in front of you. She never left you. She's been patiently waiting for you to remove the negativity from your life so that you can see just how truly beautiful you are.

Cold, Hard Stone

"The road to true love isn't always paved in gold. Sometimes, it's paved with cold, hard stone."

The truth is, sometimes the road to true love can be ugly and should you ever fall along the way, it can hurt like crazy. Just remember, it doesn't matter how much it hurts, the fall can never break you nor can it change your value. It all comes down to your perception. You see, just because you've stumbled or you've fallen doesn't mean that you are now broken nor does it mean that your journey is over. True love is still waiting for you. Understanding this will allow you to view your journey from a different perspective.

Now, with a different level of understanding, you can take that same cold, hard stone that hurt you and use it as a stepping stone to stand back up and move on.

* * * *

From this day forward, I want you to promise me, as well as yourself, that you will never again refer to yourself as being "broken." Why? Because when you do, you're saying to yourself and everyone else that you have somehow lost your value. Think of it this way... if I offered to sell you an item at its original value, but I told you it was broken, what would you think? You would probably be thinking, "No way! I'm not paying the original value for something that's already broken." Do you see where I'm going with this? By you saying that you are broken, you are essentially saying the same thing about yourself.

Now, as a result, when the Wrong Man isn't willing to give to you what you need as a Good Woman, both spiritually and emotionally to be happy in your relationship, you've preconditioned yourself to settle. Not because it's what you deserve, but because in your mind, you believe that your value has been diminished so much that you don't deserve any better.

My dear Beautiful, Strong Woman... You never lost your value. It doesn't matter what you've been through; it doesn't matter what the Wrong Man has said or done to you. You will always be worth it! Your value is non-negotiable... "NEVER AGAIN SAY I'M BROKEN!"

NOTES:

Below, I want you to write down the top 3 reasons why you see yourself as being broken.

Reason #1: _____

Reason #2: _____

Reason #3: _____

Here, I want you to write down how you felt about yourself in those areas before you felt like you had been broken.

#1: _____

_____

#2: _____

_____

#3: _____

_____

Now, I want you to look at what you have written above and understand that those beautiful things still exist within you. His words and actions may have suppressed them, but he never took them from you. He doesn't have that power.

I need you to look deep into the core of your being and find that Beautiful, Strong Woman again. You have that power... use it.

CHAPTER

Seven

THE FEAR
OF
A NEW LOVE

*"Guard your heart but don't lock it away.
Be cautious with a new love but never afraid."*

Sometimes I Wonder...

*Sometimes I wonder if some of you are trying to
convince yourself that "there are no good men"
as a defense mechanism against being disappointed...
like if he messes up, it won't hurt so much because
you never really believed things would work out
in the first place.
Or, maybe it's just easier for you to believe that
"there are no good men" than it is for you to re-examine
the type of men you are giving your time to and
making the necessary adjustments there.
Or maybe... just maybe... that's how you've
preconditioned yourself to accept less,
so that when you finally do settle,
it won't seem so bad.
After all, you did say there are no good men... right?*

Be Honest With Yourself

"The truth is...
Some of you are still under the control of the Wrong
Man of your past...You just don't realize it."

A ll of your fears, your suspicions, your hesitations, your anger... your loss in the belief of a Good Man and true love, all are fruits of the Wrong Man's past manipulations. I understand... I get it, but you have to be able to reach deep down inside into the very core of your essence and take that power back from him. Only you can do that.

It all begins with you evaluating what negative impact his past actions are having on your current behavior. Once you have identified those things, take the lessons from it and let go of the rest. Don't continue to beat yourself up over it; that will only prolong the pain. Take what you can from it and move forward. When you move past the pain... you move past him.

You Have To Believe

"It's hard for you to be open to the Right Man when you don't believe he exists in the first place."

Think of it this way: Every doctor dreamed of being a doctor and believed before they became one. Every professional athlete dreamed of being a professional athlete and believed before they became one. Dreams are pictures from God sent to you to show you your endless possibilities.

The Right Man for you does exist; you have to believe in him. Then, your actions (not wasting your time on the Wrong Man, not settling, raising your standards, and getting yourself ready, etc.) have to be consistent with attracting the Right Man for you and making that dream come true. If you can't get past the dreaming and believing stages, how do you expect for him to become your reality?

Don't Give Up

"Don't give up on love because
the Wrong Man of your past hurt you.
You do realize that is exactly what he wants you to do?"

The truth is... he doesn't want to see you happy. He wants you to be so angry and bitter that you subconsciously sabotage any chances you have at a new love by either not giving anyone a chance or by treating everyone you meet like they're him. Meanwhile, he goes on with his life, building his future with someone else, while you stay miserable and stuck in the dark memories of the past. You replay his painful words, "No one will ever want you," over and over in your head, so many times that you begin to believe it.

Now, you're doing his dirty work for him. He doesn't have to hate on you because he's convinced you to hate on yourself. Stop! I understand you're hurt; I understand you're angry and you have a right to be. All

I'm saying is that it is unfair for you to take it all out on yourself or the next man. I'm not saying to forget the lesson you've learned, I am saying apply it in a way that protects you while at the same time not contaminating your future relationship with old feelings. You have to find a balance. Will you be suspicious? Sure... just don't be paranoid.

Your Expectations Are Not Your Enemy

Some say you should go into a new relationship with "Zero expectations." I disagree...

W hy? Because that concept only works on paper. You cannot remove from your heart what your heart knows is the level of treatment you need to be happy in your relationship. You may be able to ignore it in the beginning; however, over time, if you are not getting what you need, it will begin to eat you up inside.

So I say... evaluate your expectations and make sure they are "reasonable." If they are reasonable, embrace them up front or deal with being treated like a woman who has none in the end.

Don't Let Fear Block Your Blessing

Many of you have dealt with the Wrong Man and his lies for so long that when you finally meet the Right Man, the truth sounds like a lie and sincerity feels like manipulation.

When you have been blessed enough to have met the Right Man, one who loves and respects you and treats you like you deserve to be treated, you may begin to think there has to be more to it... that things are just "too good to be true." Be careful. Your fears and suspicions could cause you to reject your blessing. Not based on who he "is" but based on your fear of who he "could be."

My dear Beautiful, Strong Woman... Rest your mind. When he's the Right Man and you feel him deep down in your soul, all you have left to do is let go; let go of your fears and let that man love you. He's trying to give you what he knows you deserve... the best of him. Let him do it.

Any Questions?

She said, "Yes... just one.
When you've been burned in the past...
when your heart has been broken to the point where you
are afraid to love again... How do you get over the fear?"

My thoughts... I believe you have to take time for yourself first. During that time, look at all the lessons of the past. Learn from them and let go of the rest; use those lessons to build a stronger, more informed "You" for the future. Once you're ready, you'll be able to move forward; however, as long as you hold on to the fear, you will stay still... even when you don't have to.

Remember, fear is based on your perception of things. If you can change the way you look at your past, you can change the way you see your future. That change will help you to go from being "fearful" to being "cautious."

Think of it like the flames on your stove; are you afraid of them or are you cautious? You know those flames could badly burn you, yet you are not afraid to cook; you are merely cautious while cooking. Even if you've been burned in the past, you don't give up on eating. Why? Because you know that food feeds the body. Well, the same applies here. You shouldn't give up on love because true love feeds the soul... just be a little more cautious.

* * * *

CHAPTER

Eight

BREATHE

My dear Beautiful, Strong Woman...
Close your eyes for a moment and just breathe.
Inhale all the strength, the power, and the courage
you need to let go and move on.
Now exhale all the pains, the frustrations,
and the sorrows that have weighed so heavily
on your heart... Just breathe.

Turn The Page

*You've been running for so long that
you're now exhausted...
Just Breathe.
You've dashed in and out of relationship after
relationship searching for the Right Man, and you still
haven't found him... Just Breathe.
So what now?
You give up and you settle.
You sacrifice who you are just to be with the Wrong
Man and to become who he wants you to be.
And you wonder why you can't sleep at night...
you wonder why your world has become so dark that
you no longer can see your own light.
My dear Beautiful Strong Woman... Just Breathe.
This may be a chapter in your life, but it is in no way,
shape or form your whole story.
Turn the page, make a change and
return yourself to glory... Just Breathe.*

He Can't Stop You

"Not even the Wrong Man can stop you from receiving your blessing. He may have been just what you needed to point you back in the right direction."

The road to your happiness is not an easy one; it takes discipline and focus. Sometimes you get tired of the journey, and you begin to think about settling for something close to what you deserve.

I believe the Wrong Man serves as a reminder to you as to why you have to keep moving forward until you reach your destination. He reminds you of the pain and the heartache of giving up and settling.

My dear Beautiful, Strong Woman, don't be discouraged. Take his lesson and use it to refocus back on the things that truly matter to you. Use it as a reminder to never again become distracted, to never again make excuses for a man you know doesn't feed your soul. Use it as a reminder to never again stop because it's easier to stop than it is to keep moving forward! Never settle; you're almost there... Stay focused!

A Clean Canvas

Clear your heart of all the anger and frustration
left by the Wrong Man of your past.
Erase his presence from your heart so that when
you meet the right artist,
you can present him with a clean canvas.
One that will allow him the freedom to
paint you a brand new picture...
one far more beautiful than anything your heart has
ever seen... unrestricted by your past and with
the limitless possibilities that only the love
of the Right Man can bring.

It's Never Too Late

*"It doesn't matter how long it's been.
It doesn't matter that you are a little bit older;
all the horrible things the Wrong Man said to you as
you walked out that door for the last time,
none of that matters. All that matters now
is that you are finally free to let the
Beautiful, Strong Woman inside of you shine."*

Don't be sad and don't be afraid. This is your moment... the moment you decide that you're not asking too much... that love, trust, and respect are not options but necessities, that quality time is important to you, and if a man can't make time, he can't have you! This is the moment that you decide that your happiness is a priority and if he can't make it his priority, then a relationship with you is no longer a possibility! This is your moment of empowerment! My dear Beautiful, Strong Woman, it's never too late for you to take control and change everything.

CHAPTER

Nine

YOU ARE STILL BEAUTIFUL... YOU ARE STILL STRONG

"One of the most beautiful sounds I have ever heard is the sound of a Beautiful, Strong Woman's voice once she has discovered her true worth. She sounds empowered, she sounds confident but most of all... she sounds free."

Know Your Worth

"Just because the Wrong Man didn't see your value,
doesn't mean you're not worth it."

Remember this: A blind man will walk past a million dollars and a foolish man will make waste of it, that doesn't change its value; it's still a million dollars.

My dear Beautiful, Strong Woman... Know your worth! Don't let their inability to see it or their lack of appreciation for it cause you to doubt your value. Regardless of their thoughts, regardless of their opinions... you will always be worth it.

Hold Your Head Up

"Though you may feel like giving up...
like the weight of the world is on your shoulders and no
one can hear your cries,
hold your head up, take in a deep breath and
just know... you can do this!"

Whatever you are going through, you can get through it. Every day, when you wake up, say to yourself, "Today, I promise to fight the urge to be totally consumed by my past and to focus on today and my future. I promise to smile, I promise to laugh, I promise to fight like crazy today so that tomorrow I can smile a little bit easier... laugh a little bit harder and be one step closer to finally being free."

You Are The Blessing

*As a Good Woman, I know sometimes you get so
frustrated that you think to yourself,
"Why should I be a Good Woman around
all of these Wrong Men?"
You wonder if it would just be easier to be like
those "other" women.
Then, maybe it wouldn't hurt so bad.
My dear Beautiful, Strong Woman...
You are who you are because when God called out,
you were one of the few who answered.
Don't turn your back now.
You are a much-needed light in a very cold and dark
space. Who you are and the one you represent
cannot be forgotten nor erased...
STAY STRONG.*

You Are Not Bound By The Limits Of A Man's Mind

Do not let anyone place limits on you.
I understand that every culture is different and
that different places have different rules;
however, I believe that your value, as a Good Woman,
doesn't change based on geography.
Some may not acknowledge your value, but that
doesn't change it. No one has the power
to change your value but you.
You see... it's not about what they say,
it's about what you believe.

She Needs To Hear It From You First

The next time you walk past the mirror,
stop for a moment and look at the woman
standing there before you and smile.
Tell her she is Beautiful...
Tell her you love her...
Tell her you are proud of her and
how far she has come. Say to her, "It doesn't matter
how much they doubt, I will always believe in you."
She needs to hear it from you before it can mean
anything coming from anyone else.

You Have To "Believe It" To "See It"

Some say,

You have to "See it" to "Believe it."

I say,

You have to "Believe it" first, before you can "See it."

So Believe!

Believe that you are Beautiful...

Believe that you are Strong...

Believe that you are truly worthy of all the love
and respect that a Good Woman deserves.

Believe it!

Timelessly Beautiful

There is no need for you to feel self-conscious
about any part of your body.
The only reason you see these parts as being imperfect is
that you've been taught to believe true beauty cannot be
fully achieved until you look like someone else who society
says is beautiful... I disagree.
I believe true beauty comes from the fact that you were
perfectly made by the hands of He who is much greater
than any man. That, in and of itself, makes you more
beautiful than anything man himself could ever create.
So I say, embrace your uniqueness and know that there
has never been and there will never be another
just like you; you are a once in forever, and that is what
makes you... timelessly beautiful.

Worthy Of The Sacrifice

You are still beautiful...
from the top of your head to the bottom of your feet...
From the sound of your voice
to the way that you think.
It's everything about you
that makes you beautifully unique.
My dear Beautiful, Strong Woman...
If love was a mountain,
the Right Man for you would climb to the very peak.
And when he finally reached the top,
exhausted yet still on his feet,
then and only then can you trust and believe that
you are in the presence of a man who
is willing to sacrifice everything just to prove his love to you.

Remember Your Dream

You all have a dream...
something that was born in you as a little girl and
still burns at the very core of your soul.
What is it?

S ome of you may have forgotten. I'm here to remind you. Find a quiet place, close your eyes and listen. Listen to her laugh. Listen to her sing; remember how it felt for you as a little girl just to dream. What does that dream look like? How does that dream feel and are you working towards it or against it? You don't have to answer right now; I just want you to think about it.

What Is Your Purpose?

My dear Beautiful, Strong Woman...
What is your purpose?
Why are you here?
So many didn't make it to see today,
but yet you did. Why?
There is something great inside each and every one of you.
You all have a beautiful purpose.
Do you know what that purpose is?
I believe I have found mine;
It took me a while, but I believe I have found it.
Tell me, what's in your heart?
What is your purpose?

Admired From Afar

Some of you have been through it all...
disappointments, heartbreak, betrayal... everything.
Some nights, as I sit and write and I read hundreds of
your comments, I wonder how you do it.
The strength it must take to keep standing back up,
day after day, holding your head up high
and refusing to be broken.
You are truly inspiring.
I watch you from afar, and though I do not know
who you are, I admire you.
I admire your strength;
I admire your courage, I admire the very essence of
what you represent:
the Beautiful, Strong Woman.

Between You & I

I don't want to motivate you,
I want to inspire you...
Inspire you to look within and find your inner greatness...
to remind you of your true strength
so that long after my last thought has been spoken
and the last page has been turned,
you will forever know that
you are a Beautiful, Strong Woman
and no one can ever take that away from you.
No one.

™

CHAPTER

Ten

THE
GOOD
WOMAN

The Right Man's Rock

A Good Woman will stand by the Right Man for her
even if he loses everything (job, house, car, career, etc.)
because she knows, as long as he doesn't
lose himself in the process,
he has the power to rebuild it; it's in his DNA.
That's one of the things that attracted her to
him in the first place.

Every man, at some point, gets knocked down. If he hasn't been knocked down at least once, he hasn't been trying hard enough. The real question is whether or not he gets back up. If he doesn't, that man will no longer be an asset to you, he'll be a liability. In time, your love will turn into frustration, and you'll eventually lose respect for him.

But a good, strong man, he's a different story. He has the power to make the sequel better than the original story and you know it. That's one of the qualities that you love so much about him.

She Refuses To Play The "Game"

Some believe a Good Woman
needs to learn to play some sort of "game"
in order to get a Good Man.
My thoughts...
I believe if you, the Good Woman, stay true to
your essence, the Right Man will one day come into
your life and love and cherish you the way you deserve.
Not because you learned to play the "game,"
but because you've stayed true to who you are and
unlike so many others, you refuse to play it.
That's what makes you so special.
Be patient... Never settle.

A Generous Heart

"A Good Woman's love is so generous that, even when she has nothing, she is willing to try to create something if it will help the man she truly loves."

If he's the Right Man, this quality could be one of your greatest strengths. If he's the Wrong Man, it might prove to be one of your greatest weaknesses. This is why you choosing the Right Man is so important. As a Good Woman, your heart won't let you standby and watch him struggle, it will force you to do something to try and help him. You want to make sure you've made a good selection so when and if that time ever comes, you're helping the Right Man and not being used by the wrong one.

Imperfect Yet Always Worth It

*"As a Good Woman, you won't always be perfect,
but in the eyes and heart of the Right Man,
you will always be worth it."*

A Good Woman is irreplaceable and the Right Man knows it. He knows that there are many substitutes; however, there is no worthy replacement for the real thing. To him, you are the real thing. You are worthy of the sacrifice, worthy of all the loyalty, love and respect that his heart can give. In his mind... he has no doubt.

The Power To Transform

Don't let the Wrong Man's wrongs take away from you
one of the most precious things about you...
your belief in true love.
A Good Woman's true love is powerful to
the Right Man... it is transforming.
It has the power to make the Right Man stand up and
continue even when he feels that he can continue no more.
In the old days, we fought for it.
Today, there are no duels, there are no fights to the death.
Today, the Right Man simply humbles himself, bows his
head and prays for it.
I pray that you never change that about you.

A Moment Of Clarity

I've been asked what do I mean when I say,
"A Good Woman."
My dear Beautiful, Strong Woman... I mean be "You."
Honest and pure, imperfect, yet perfectly "You."
Unaffected by the lost morals of the world and truly
connected to your spiritual essence.
You are truly a beautiful being;
embrace that about you.
It won't be easy, but that's what makes your heart such
a beautiful place of peace in a world that is such a mess.
When I say, "A Good Woman,"
I am referring to the Beautiful, Strong Woman
that lives inside of you.

CHAPTER
Eleven
KNOWING
THE
DIFFERENCE

*Sometimes, you knowing the difference can make
all the difference in the world.*

Playing House

Some men want to "Play House."
They want to be in a relationship
but don't want to spend any time with you.
They want to sleep with you
but don't want to commit to you.
They want all the benefits
without any of the responsibilities.
The Right Man; however,
is not about "Playing House,"
he's about working with you to build one.
A place of peace and security where all of your
worries stop at the front door.
The Right Man is looking to create a love so real that
you will feel his heart worthy enough to
make it your home.

Does He "Add To" Or "Take Away" From Your Happiness

"The Right Man for you will add to your happiness...
The Wrong Man will consistently take away from it."

The key part here is "consistently take away from it." Think about it... every relationship has its ups and downs, that's normal. However, if the majority of your days are spent crying or upset because of what he has said to you or because of the way you are being treated, you may want to rethink whether or not he is the Right Man for you.

My thoughts... when a man truly loves you, he builds you up, he doesn't spend his time consistently trying to break you down.

Share The Burden

Ladies...
The Right Man will share the burden...
The Wrong Man will become one.

Have you ever been doing just fine for yourself and then met a man and all of a sudden life just became difficult... like the only thing he brought to the relationship was extra baggage that he now expected you to carry? Some of you have been there; some of you are still there now.

My advice: Stop carrying these grown men! The longer you carry him, the weaker he'll become. At the end of the day, you'll be left with a Weak Man who will depend on you for everything. The sad part about it is, the longer you carry him, the more obligated you will feel to continue. Is that what you really want? Just something for you to think about.

Ready Or Not

My dear Beautiful, Strong Woman...
You should not accept any man as "your man" until he
shows you that he is ready to accept all the
responsibilities that come with that position.

The Right Man knows that it's not about who can get the most women, it's about who can prepare himself, as a man, well enough to make one Good Woman want to stay... that's the key.

Remember, you are not the same as the rest of them... you're different. The Right Man for you will not be simply looking for a "good time." He's looking to commit to you and to provide stability, trust, loyalty, love, and respect. If a man is not willing to give you these things, he's simply not ready for you.

™

CHAPTER

Twelve

REMEMBER
THIS...

Who he "Is" and who you "Want him to be"
are sometimes two different people.
You can't blame him for being the man he chooses to be.
You can only make a decision as to whether or not
the man he chooses to be is the man you want in your life.

Chemistry

My dear Beautiful, Strong Woman,
Remember this...
Chemistry does not equal "Love."
Chemistry does not equal "Loyalty."
Chemistry does not equal "Trust or Commitment."
Chemistry equals "Attraction."
Attraction without love, loyalty, trust and
commitment equals absolutely nothing.
In the end, chemistry may be what initially
brings you two together,
but it's the love, loyalty, trust, and commitment
that will keep things from falling apart.

The Painful Truth About Sex

"If he wants sex and you want a relationship,
it will seldom work out for you in the end.
Why?
Because regardless of whether or not you give him
what he wants, he will never give you what you want."

My dear Beautiful, Strong Woman, here is the painful truth: If all he wants is sex, you giving it to him won't magically make him want a relationship. It just doesn't work that way. He may stay for a time; however, when he has grown tired, bored or someone new comes along, he'll be on his way and there will be nothing you can do to stop him. Why? Because he will have already gotten what he wanted from you and, in his mind, there will be no reason to stay.

By the same token, if all he wants is sex and you don't

give it to him, eventually he'll seek it from someone else. Not because you are any less of a woman, but simply because he was never interested in being in a relationship with you in the first place. He was only interested in the sex, and where the sex is, he is sure to follow.

My thoughts... this is why it is so important for you to take your time to gain a greater understanding of the man you are dealing with. If you want love, respect, and commitment, settle for nothing less than a man who is willing to give you those things. Never think that sex alone will eventually lead to it; you will only be fooling yourself.

When He Won't Listen

"A man who is unwilling to listen,
is a man who is unwilling to change."

When He Does Listen But Doesn't Care

*"Sometimes, him listening isn't the issue,
it's his reason for listening that causes the problem."*

The Wrong Man will listen to you; however, he'll be more concerned with what his answer will be rather than what you are actually saying. Remember, when he's wrong, he doesn't care about what you have to say or how you feel, it's all about him.

The Right Man; however, will listen to you first and foremost to gain a better understanding of you and your perspective. For him, how you feel, your mental and your emotional health are important. He knows that the better he understands you, the better the chances that his response will be more conducive to a solution rather than it adding to the problem.

The Man Stuck In The Middle

*"How can one man be so right,
yet so wrong for you, all at the same time."*

The most confusing man you will ever meet is the one who is still in the middle. He's both the Wrong Man and the Right Man in one man; he's both the good and the bad, your brightest moments and your darkest hours. He's the first to make you laugh and the first to make you cry. This is the man you'll have the hardest time understanding because, on the one hand, you love him for the joy, but on the other hand, you despise him for the pain.

So what do you do? How long are you willing to stay on his emotional roller coaster before it makes you sick to your stomach? One month, two months... two years? How long before you realize that you can't do this forever... that it is literally making you sick inside. How long?

Remember, no man is perfect. In the end, the Right Man for you may sometimes make you mad, but he should never make you sick.

The Truth About Time

Time is both your best friend and your worst enemy.
Your best friend because you need time to
determine whether or not he's the Right Man for you...
Your worst enemy because within that
same time period, if you're not careful, by the time you
realize he's the Wrong Man for you,
you will have already developed feelings for him that
are hard to walk away from.

My thoughts... be cautious as to how much you bring down your walls during the initial dating period. Remember, most of the time, the Wrong Man is not going to just present himself as the Wrong Man upfront; he will do it gradually over a period of time. You have to pay attention. I'm not saying you should be cold or totally disconnected during this time; I am saying understand this dynamic and carefully balance your actions accordingly.

His Attention

"The one thing you should never have to fight for is his attention."

When he's the Wrong Man for you, you'll find yourself consistently competing with everyone and everything else. You'll become so frustrated because as a Good Woman, you're willing to make sure that he knows he is a priority in your life, but he can never do the same for you.

The Right Man; however, will never make you

consistently fight for his attention; he'll do his best to make sure that you always know that you are a priority in his life. This doesn't mean that other things won't ever come up that require his focus or his attention, it simply means that when those things do come up, because he has been consistent and has communicated to you the change in events, you two remain on the same page and there is no reason for you to doubt.

Sometimes "Sorry" Just Isn't Enough

Some men believe that just because they apologize, they are instantly entitled to your trust again.
I disagree...

If he has done something that has totally ruined your trust in him, you should not be expected to act as if nothing has happened nor should you feel obligated to instantly trust him again. He should have to work to rebuild your trust.

If he's not willing to put in the work, that apology was not sincere, and he's not serious about moving forward.

Revenge Is Not Always Sweet

You could be upset... You could be frustrated...
You could be so angry that you could scream
at the top of your lungs...
so loud that the world itself would feel your pain, but
what you should never do is do to the Wrong Man
what he has done to you.
Why?
Because if you do,
you become that which you so despise.

You Are Not Paranoid

If you don't trust anyone or anything else,
trust the voice inside of you;
it's there for a reason.
The Wrong Man may tell you that you are being
"Paranoid" or that it is just your "Imagination," but
deep down inside...
You know it's much more than that.

Energy speaks much louder than words. When that feeling inside is so strong that you just can't ignore it, when it chases you in your dreams and it just won't let you rest... when it twists and turns deep down in your stomach until you literally begin to feel physically sick, don't ignore it. It's trying to tell you something.

Intuition

My dear Beautiful, Strong Woman...
You have been blessed with the gift of having a
divine connection to a power much greater than
your own, yet you choose to ignore it.
Instead, you choose to believe the words from the
very tongue that your divine connection was meant to
protect you from... Why?
Is your addiction to love so strong that even when he's
wrong, you can still see right...
that even when it's dark, you can still see the light
from the infinite possibilities that his love could bring if
he would just do right?
YES, you all say!
Just know that what the Wrong Man calls love
you call pain and if you would just close your eyes and
listen for a moment, you would hear your intuition has
been trying to tell you the very same thing.

Real Change

Real change in a man takes time.
If you ever break up and he immediately comes back to
you saying he's changed... be cautious.

That kind of change usually only lasts a few days... maybe a few weeks or a few months, then you're right back where you started.

Think about it for a minute... In the past, when you have broken it off more than 1 or 2 times with the same man, it's usually for similar behavior. That's because he never really changed. He said what he thought you wanted to hear and once he had you back, he could only keep the act up for so long before the same man you broke up with began to show up again.

My thoughts... trust your intuition. If you don't believe he's already changed (not still in the process of changing, but already changed) be careful. The flame that burned you in the past still burns. Are you willing to continue to play with fire?

Never Beg

My dear Beautiful, Strong Woman,
Remember this...
Never beg a man to stay.
Why beg him to stay when his heart
has already decided to leave?
Are you willing to settle simply for his presence
knowing deep down inside that his heart is
no longer yours?
No! You deserve much better than that.
You deserve someone who doesn't have to
be begged to stay because they love and cherish you so
much that they would never even dream of leaving.
No... If that man wants to leave, let him go.
Never beg.

His Journey

The Wrong Man will only begin his journey towards
being the Right Man when he's ready.
Sometimes, losing you, the Good Woman, is necessary
to convince him to take his first step.

Think about this for a moment: When you lose something and you are able to get it back, that's a learning experience. When you lose something that you can never get back, that's a lifelong lesson. Sometimes it takes a lifelong lesson to convince a man to change his life.

Part II
For Him

CHAPTER

Thirteen

A TIME
TO REFLECT

"She's tried talking to you, but you won't listen.
She's cried herself to sleep at night,
but you're not paying attention.
She's tried everything in her power to get you to
show her that you still care. The sad part about it is...
you may not see it until she's no longer there."

Blind To The Signs

You walk in and out of the house,
and you still don't see it.
The pain in her eyes, the sadness in her voice,
the change in her posture...
it's all right there, staring you in the face,
and yet you still don't see it.
You are so focused on "You" that you
don't even see her anymore.
You look past her as you walk by, totally consumed
with what it takes to be a provider,
not realizing that you are slowly losing the one person
that you are trying to provide for.

My thoughts... find a balance. You being a successful provider does not have to come at her expense. You can be successful at what you do and still have a healthy relationship with her. It's about balance. Find a balance that works for both of you.

...*Before It's Too Late*

When she brings it up once,
you say she's complaining.
When she brings it up twice,
you say she's nagging.
When she cries about it,
you say she's being too sensitive.
My good friend, let me ask you this,
when she leaves... what will she be then?

Think about this for a minute... Why? Because we sometimes don't give this process any thought until we're at the final question and by then, it's often gotten so bad that it's almost impossible to fix.

My hope is that if you're somewhere before the end, you'll stop and address the issue before it's too late.

Between The Lines

She was in love with you,
but you were too busy playing games to see it.
She would have done anything for you,
but your ego was so big that you had convinced yourself
that you didn't need that. Now that she's long gone and
you've finished beating on your chest and telling all your
friends about how you could care less,
the day has finally come, and you are starting to realize
that you let the best thing to ever happen to you go...
like footprints covered by the winter snow, she's gone.
And you have no one to blame but yourself.

As men, we don't always like to admit that sometimes, we regret being the man we once were... that there are times when we wish we had the chance to do it all over again. If we could, we'd do it differently.

That's a confession that the Good Woman of the past may never hear, but between you and I... we know.

My Loss...
Our Lesson

She said, "You never listened to me."
I said, "I did listen to you."
She said, "You stopped paying attention to me."
I said, "I never stopped paying attention to you."
She said, "Then why, when I reached out to you about
what I needed, nothing ever changed...
why, when I laid down next to you,
could you not feel my pain?"
I was speechless.

My Good Friend... sometimes we think we're listening, but are we really listening? We think we're paying attention, but are we really paying attention? I only ask because I've had to ask myself the very same question, and the answer was a very hard pill to swallow. So, today I leave this with you in hopes that my loss can be our lesson.

Seasons Change...
So Can We

The strange thing is...
Sometimes, we as men, work so hard to get her
and then we do nothing to make her want to stay.
Then, when we lose her,
we're back to trying to do everything to get her back.

The question is, why should she take you back? What do you plan to do differently this time around? Why should she believe you... simply because you say it? Remember, that's exactly what you said in the first place. Why should she believe this time will be any different?

I only say this to say, when trying to get her back, your words mean nothing; it's all in your actions. Why? Because it was your actions or lack of action that caused you to lose her in the first place.

NOTES:

Write down 3 things that you believe, if you improved about yourself, would enhance the chances of your relationship being successful. Think through this and don't let the thought of "this is just the way I am" stop you from reflecting and being open to change in those areas.

1. _____

_____

2. _____

_____

3. _____

_____

Remember... we are who we are because that is who we choose to be. There's nothing wrong with you choosing to be a better version of "You."

TM

CHAPTER

Fourteen

A NEW
LEVEL OF
UNDERSTANDING

"A Good Woman is not interested in your
money or your status.
What she wants from you is your time,
loyalty, love and commitment."

The Truth Is...

A Good Woman is not that complicated.

T he complication comes from some men lacking the patience, or the desire, or the discipline it takes to really get to know her and truly understand her.

It's like trying to understand a 300-page book simply by reading the summary. You may learn her highlights, but you will never truly know her story... not until you sit down and actually take the time to get to know her.

She Wants
A Man Of Purpose

A Good Woman isn't interested in "dating"
just for the sake of "dating."
She wants to be courted by a man with
a genuine heart and an honorable purpose.
In her eyes, her time is precious, and she sees no value in
simply dating a man who has no purpose.

Consistency Over Time

"She doesn't want you to try to impress her by doing all
these wonderful things in the beginning, knowing
you have no intention of continuing them once she's
fallen for you; that's false advertising."

She Needs More From You

You want to give her your time,
but only on the weekends.
She needs more from you.
You want to buy her a beautiful dress,
but you're never around to see her wear it.
She needs more from you.
Your text messages are nice... but she needs more.
Your late night calls give her hope,
but she knows that talking to you on the phone
means you're not there with her.
She needs more from you.
You see, she longs for your presence, not your presents.
If you ask her, a Good Woman will tell you that
all those other things are nice,
but all she's ever really wanted was you.

Time Spent

*"Just because you spent time with her yesterday,
doesn't mean it's okay to neglect her today."*

To put it simply, it's about balance and you gaining a deeper understanding of the emotional needs of the woman you are with. Every woman is different; however, there aren't too many women out there who will be okay with being totally neglected for an entire day. She may act as if it doesn't bother her the first few times, but if quality time is important to her, she won't be able to ignore that feeling forever. In your mind, you may be thinking that since you spent the entire day with her yesterday, she should be okay with you doing your thing all day today. My friend, that may sound good; however, it will seldom work out that way.

My thoughts... find out what her emotional needs

are, as it relates to time spent, and go off of that. She may only require a simple phone call or a text; she may need additional face-to-face time. Whatever that need is, it is up to you to learn it and make the necessary adjustments to meet it. Don't go based on what you did with your last girlfriend. If you do, you'll have a 50/50 chance of being dead wrong. Instead, learn the woman you are with now and raise those odds to you having a 100% chance of being right.

Why She's Upset

*"She's not upset that you don't agree with her;
she's upset that whenever you do disagree with her,
your tone is condescending and you minimize
her opinion. To disagree is understandable...
to disregard her feelings and act as if her opinion
doesn't matter is unacceptable."*

Just Fix It

"Don't apologize and then continue to do the same thing over and over again... Just fix it."

We all make mistakes; that's understandable, but just know that if you keep doing the same thing over and over again and keep apologizing for it, your subsequent apologies will not make things any better, they will only make things worse. Why? Because she knows that if you were truly sorry, there would be no need to keep apologizing; you would have already fixed the problem. Now, your subsequent apologies are beginning to insult her. She's not only hurt that you did what you did, but she's also angry and frustrated that you keep on apologizing and still nothing changes. In short, you've aggravated the first problem and created a second one.

My thoughts... if you have done something to the woman you love and you are truly sorry and feel she deserves an apology, then she also deserves for you to take the time to correct the problem. I know it's hard to set aside the ego sometimes, but think of it this way... your ego will always be there, but if you don't make this right, she might not be.

Understanding Her Is Part Of The Solution

"She's not always looking for you to find the solution for her; sometimes, all she needs is to be heard and to know that you understand her."

Sometimes we, as men, get caught up in the logical part of the conversation. We focus only on the solution, and we fail to see the emotional aspects of the issue and how they are affecting her. When we ignore those aspects of it, we often come across as being emotionally cold and insensitive.

My thoughts... maybe there is a better way; maybe

the answer lies, not so much in the solution itself, but in our understanding of the effect the issue has on her emotionally. By first showing that you understand, maybe that would reduce her feelings of frustration and allow her to ultimately be more open to you working with her on the solution.

Knowing Your Role

As her man, she needs you to know your role.

*When it rains and she needs you to be strong,
she expects you to bring an umbrella to
protect her from the rain.
However, when it rains and she needs you to be
supportive, she expects you to take her by the hand
and dance with her in it.
It's up to you to learn her well enough to know when to
dance in it and when to protect her from it.
In the end, it's not about being able to read her mind,
it's about you taking the time to truly get to know her.*

Listen To Her

Listen to her...
When she walks into the room and says nothing...
Listen to her.
When she climbs into bed, curls up on her side and
says nothing... Listen to her.
When she calls you on the phone and
is unusually quiet... Listen to her.
She's calling out to you emotionally in a voice
you'll never hear if you only listen with your ears;
you have to listen with your heart.
When you do, not only will you hear her,
but you'll feel her as well.
Now, all you have to do is stop whatever it is you're
doing and answer her call.

If you pay attention to her, you'll learn so much more through her behavior. Sometimes, she doesn't want to bother you. You have to be able to sense those times and let her know that she's not bothering you and that you're interested in what's going on with her. Just that feeling of her knowing you are there for her is often enough to make her feel better about whatever it is she's going through.

Getting Past Your Fears

When you have a Good Woman,
you have to be able to let go of your fears, set aside your
ego and allow her to love you with all her heart,
mind, body and soul.
When you do, her love has the absolute power to,
not only bring out the best in you, but it has the power
to change your whole life perspective.
You just have to be open to changing
the way you think about love.
Let go of the idea that to love a Good Woman is to
be weak, and embrace the idea that a Good Woman's
love is actually a critical element to the true strength
and power of a Good Man.

CHAPTER
Fifteen
EXPRESS
YOURSELF

She won't see it if you don't show her...
She won't know it if you don't tell her.

No More Assumptions

As men, we sometimes assume.
We assume that the Beautiful, Strong Woman in each
of our lives knows that we think about her all the time...
We assume that even when we don't say it, they know
that we love them... We assume.
We assume they know that we think
they look beautiful even when they are having
one of those days and they just don't feel that way...
We assume.

In all honesty, I think we all can admit that at times, we can be a bit guilty of this. We walk into a room and see that she has on a new outfit or that she has done something different to her hair and, in our minds, we're thinking, "Wow, she looks amazing," but we don't verbalize it nor do our actions show her what we are actually thinking. Instead, we walk out of the room still thinking she looks amazing while she stands there feeling totally invisible, disappointed and let down.

Why? Because in her mind, we didn't even notice.

My thoughts... when you think it, say it. Find a way to express the thought in both a verbal and physical form. You'll be amazed at what a simple sign of recognition will do for her.

With that being said, today, we throw away all assumptions, and we find the time to tell the Beautiful, Strong Woman in each of our lives, just how beautiful and truly amazing she is.

Remind Her Today...

We, as men, don't often say what a difference a Good Woman's love has made in our lives. We sort of keep on moving forward with the relationship without ever actually telling her.
My friend, for you to talk to her about how you feel is not a show of weakness. It is, in her eyes, your greatest show of strength. If you haven't had that conversation with her, I am sure she would love to hear it from you. If you already have... remind her today.

Take Pride In Her

*There's nothing wrong with you telling her that
you are proud of her.
There's nothing wrong with you letting her know
you are proud of all she has accomplished.
There's nothing wrong with you telling her
you are proud of the Beautiful, Strong Woman
she's become... that you are proud of
everything about her.
Most of all, there's nothing wrong with you telling her
that you are proud to be her man.
There's nothing wrong with telling her.*

Show Her

You say that you love her...
then show her.
And don't show her the way "You" feel she should be loved.
Show her the way "She" feels she needs to be loved.
Once you've taken the time to learn and understand her,
you'll understand this and things will make
so much more sense.

Y ou see, sometimes it has nothing to do with her being unreasonable or expecting too much; sometimes, it has to do with you simply putting all your energy into the wrong things. Not because those things aren't genuinely your expression of true love, but more often than not, it's because those things simply aren't what she needs to feel loved and appreciated.

Now, I know you may be thinking, "I'm not a mind

reader; I've tried everything. How am I supposed to express to her my love if nothing I do seems to work?"

My good friend, the answer is simple... throw away everything you think would work and start all over with a clean canvas. Remember, she's unique and everything that may have worked in your past relationships may not work with her today.

Talk to her. Watch her. Listen to her. If you pay close enough attention, she'll tell you exactly what it is she needs from you. Whether it be more quality time or something as simple as holding her hand; it could be a five minute phone call when you wake up and right before you go to bed just to let her know that she's both the first thing on your mind in the morning and the last thing on your mind at night. Whatever it is, if you pay close attention, she'll tell you.

Now, it's up to you to be open to a new way of expressing your love to her. It may feel a little different at first, but after a while, it will become second nature to you.

In the end, your new expressions of love will be better received by her, and she'll feel more confident and secure about how you feel about her and the state of your relationship.

Your Emotional Connection

The power is in your gaze...
As you look into her eyes and say everything your heart
feels without ever saying one word.
She feels like...
at that very moment, you said so much,
and even though nothing was heard,
she felt everything.
You see, that's the true power of emotionally connecting
with a Good Woman.
When you learn to communicate in her language,
she begins to understand you better;
she begins to love you better.
When you can remove all doubt from her mind,
a Good Woman will love you forever.

Do You Remember...

My Good Friend...
Do you remember the very first day you realized
you truly loved her...
that it was no longer a game and that she was the one?
Where were you?
What were you doing?
Have you ever sat down and told her how,
at that very moment, she had done what no other
woman could do?
That she made you understand being vulnerable to her
was not a weakness, but rather it was your
greatest demonstration of strength, confidence and
conviction... that for you to trust her meant you were
strong enough to overcome your fears and confident
enough to trust in her to always have your back.
Have you ever sat down and had
that conversation with her?
That's something she needs to hear from you.

Final Thoughts

Early morning kisses...
best way to send her off to work.

Midday call or text...
best way to remind her that she is always on your mind.

Evening kisses, open ears, and back rubs...
best way to welcome her home.

My point...
Don't make it more complicated than it really is.
Some days it really is just this simple.

I n the end, find a way to express to her how you truly feel about her. Whether it's one of the above-mentioned methods or something totally different, whatever it is... express yourself.

Part III
For Both Of You

CHAPTER

Sixteen

MAKING IT
WORK II

Even if it's "meant to be,"
you'll still have to work at it to make it work.

Overcoming The Fear
Of Being Hurt

*So many Good Women have dealt with the Wrong
Man, and so many Good Men have dealt with the
Wrong Woman that, by the time you two finally meet,
you're both afraid of each other...
so afraid, you run the risk of ending it before
you've even given it a chance.*

The problem is that so many of you are afraid of
getting hurt that you don't give your relationship
your all. When one of you doesn't give it your
all, the other person feels it and begins to question your
commitment to the relationship. Then, they too become
afraid of getting hurt and begin to hold back as well.

Now, you begin to feel like something isn't right and

begin holding back even more. Do you see where this is going? Pretty soon, both of you are holding back so much that neither one of you are giving the relationship anything it needs to grow and it begins to die. Not because it can't work, but because one or both of you are so afraid of getting hurt that you stop trying to make it work altogether.

My thoughts... let that fear go. You will never know the true potential of your relationship if one or both of you continue to carry it around. It will eventually weigh you both down.

In the end, if you two have taken the time to really get to know each other and both of you are truly interested in creating something absolutely amazing together, you have to be able to trust each other. You can't allow your past relationships to contaminate your present one. Take the lessons and leave the rest. If this relationship is what you want, you have to trust that giving the other person your all is not a gamble but a worthy investment... that they have your back and you have theirs. You both just have to be willing to push through it. If you two can push through it together, you can make it work, but it's going to take both of you.

It Takes Two

As a Good Woman, you have to be able to
talk to your man so he can better understand you.
And he has to be willing to listen.
At the same time,
you also have to be willing to listen to him.
Remember, it takes two.

I f he understands you perfectly, yet you have no understanding of him, what have you accomplished? Yes, you may feel better; however, he now feels miserable. That will get you the same heartbreaking results.

My dear Beautiful, Strong Woman... the same way you need to be heard and feel understood by him, he needs to be heard and feel like he's understood by you.

In the end, for it to work, it will take both of you listening, understanding, and putting into action all the things necessary to keep things moving forward.

The Tough Times

When things get tough, don't just give up on each other.
If the love is there...
if the respect is there...
if you two are still committed to each other
and want it to work,
don't just walk away.
As long as you fight together, anything is possible.
If one or both of you stops...
all will be lost.

Drifting Apart Doesn't "Just Happen"

I often hear people say,
"Over time... we just drifted apart."
My thoughts...
No, time alone didn't do that.
Time is simply a convenient scapegoat.
The truth is, over time, one or both of you stopped doing
the things that brought you together and kept you
together in the first place.
There is where the problem lies.

In a relationship, people don't "just" drift apart; time alone doesn't cause that. It's what you both choose to do with your time that determines the ultimate outcome. If you stop communicating, if you stop spending time together, if one or both of you stop building upon the foundation that created the connection in the first place... you "WILL" begin to drift apart. Not simply because of "time" alone, but because of how one or both of you chose to use that time.

Relationships were never meant to work on autopilot; they're meant to be engaging. Think about it: For those of you who have a higher belief, you didn't just pray one day and find that was enough to keep your spiritual connection in good health for a lifetime. No, you are constantly working to stay in harmony with your faith and to build upon it every single day.

Your personal relationship is similar. You can't say that since you are now together, all the work is done. You have to stay focused and constantly work to stay in harmony with each other. Some may think that a relationship should not take that much work... that if it's "meant to be, it will be." I've got news for you... even those things that are "meant to be" take a lot of work.

For you two to maintain a healthy and growing relationship, it's going to take a lot of hard work, discipline, focus, and commitment. The work just gets easier when you are working together and not against each other.

You Need Each Other

Some might say,
"If a Good Woman really loves her man,
she will never give up.
She will keep fighting to make it work, no matter what."
My thoughts...
If a man truly loves you, he won't make you fight alone.
He'll be right there working with you, side by side,
to make it work because he knows
it's not just your responsibility, nor is it solely his.
The responsibility belongs to both of you.
If either one of you thinks fighting alone is enough
to save it, you are setting yourself up for heartbreak.
Whether you are the Good Man or the Good Woman,
just know...
you need each other to make it work.

It Will Work

If the two of you want it to work...
If the two of you believe it can work...
If the two of you simply decide to make it work
and refuse to let anything or anyone stand in your way,
IT WILL WORK.
You may not always agree, and some days may be
harder than others, but if you both are consistent with
your love, respect, and commitment
to each other and the relationship...
IT WILL WORK.
Some believe "what happens...happens."
I disagree.
You two can make a decision to make it work,
or one or both of you can stand by and watch it fail,
but nothing "just happens."
It's up to you...
Together, the two of you have that power.

™

CHAPTER

Seventeen

INTIMATE
MOMENTS

She just wants you to make her feel special...
Whether it's a random compliment, a glance that says,
"I think the world of you" or
you simply sitting down next to her
and placing your hand on hers. Whatever it is you do,
she's looking forward to you creating those
small moments that she can carry in her heart forever.

Your Undivided Attention

You don't need a lot of money to be romantic;
You don't need a fancy car to take her to
a place she's never been.
Can't you see, all she needs is you.
She would walk to the park just to sit on a bench
next to you if it meant she could have you all to herself
for that brief moment in time...
no cell phones, no social media... nothing.
Just you giving her 100% of your undivided attention.
Remember...
a Good Woman loves you for "who you are"
and not for "what you have."
For her, it sometimes can be just that simple.

"That" Is Why She Loves You

She loves it when you do "That."
So, what is "That?"

"That" is the compliment you give her
when she least expects it.
"That" is the passionate look you give her when
you think she's not looking but she is.
"That" is the calming tone of voice you use when
she is so upset that she just can't see straight.
"That" is the gentleness of your touch that lets her know
everything is going to be okay.
"That" is the love and respect you show her
in everything you do, every single day.
"That" is why she loves you so much
and she prays "That" will never change.

Surprises

Don't have roses delivered to her job,
surprise her by showing up and bring them
to her yourself,
along with a vase and a card;
then kiss her on her forehead and tell her
to have an amazing day.
Don't say anything else after that,
simply turn around and walk away.
Now, before those elevator doors close,
you'll catch a glimpse of that look on her face as
she smiles from ear to ear because her man just
walked in and in 30 seconds or less...
took her breath away.

Two Beautiful Minds Connected

Have you ever wondered...
at the end of the day, as she lies there on the bed
staring at the ceiling...
what runs through her mind?
What are her thoughts,
her dreams, her hopes... her fears?
What are the things that make her smile
simply by just thinking about them?
Have you ever wondered...
what runs through her mind?
My thoughts...
As she lies there, lay down next to her
and stare at the ceiling with her.
Then, gently ask her,
"My dear Beautiful, Strong Woman...
What runs through your mind?"

Every Beauty Needs Her Beast

Stop her in the hallway,
pin her up against the wall with
her hands over her head, and kiss her like you've never
kissed her before. Then walk away and
tell her that she still brings out the beast in you.

There is a fire in your passion... there is a magic in your spontaneous act of intimacy.

When she's your woman and she least expects it, show her that she still ignites that fire in you; let her know that she still has that power. Trust me when I say that by doing this, you will in turn ignite a fire inside of her that will remind her of the fact that, in your eyes, she hasn't lost it... that the passion is still there, the attraction is still there and that she still has the power to bring the beast out of you.

When The Day Is Finally Over

When the day is finally over,
nothing would make her happier than to be able to
lay her head on your chest
and fall asleep to the sound of the heartbeat
of the man she knows truly loves and adores her.

Sometimes, simply lying there doing nothing can mean absolutely everything.

Intimacy doesn't always have to be physical or about her bringing out the "beast" in you. Sometimes, it's about two souls bringing a feeling of inner peace to each other that can't be found any place else in the world; it's about connecting on a spiritual level with the one you love and adore. Sometimes, it's just that easy.

NOTES:

In closing, I know that I don't have all the answers, but sometimes it's not about me giving you the answers; sometimes, you both already have them. All you need is a spark to ignite the conversation that has for too long gone silent. In some cases, all it takes is that one conversation to put things back on track.

Below, I've given you a place to start... the rest is up to you.

_____

_____

_____

_____

_____

_____

Part IV
My Final Chapter

CHAPTER

Eighteen

NAKED

Sometimes...
the only thing strong enough to humble
a strong man is the hand of God.
It's at that very moment... the moment when
God breaks him down to his very essence,
that a man becomes emotionally open.
The ego, if only for a second,
has been defeated and that man's spirit is
completely accessible, without interference.
My dear Beautiful, Strong Woman,
Welcome to My Final Chapter... "NAKED"

The Rebirth
Of A Man

I fell from the sky and landed
less than the man I was.
And though I was buried beneath the sands,
you still extended your hand.
Your voice...
as gentle as the summer breeze.
Your love...
the very thing I needed.
My dear Beautiful, Strong Woman...
I owe you more than you will ever know...
more than my words can ever show.

Silent Conversations

If only your walls could speak.
How many times would they tell me that they
have had to stand by helplessly and watch as
you cried yourself to sleep?
If only your walls could speak.
What would they tell me about the true heartache
and the true struggles of the Good Woman?
What things could they help me to better understand,
as a man, and what changes would it bring?
If only your walls could speak...
I wonder what they would say to me.

No More Secrets

You say that you don't care, but
I know that you do.
You say that it doesn't matter, but
I know that it does.
My dear Beautiful, Strong Woman...
You cannot hide it from me.
I close my eyes, and I feel what you deny;
I feel everything that you hide.
Is that my greatest blessing or my greatest curse,
as a man, to feel you when it hurts...
to understand you at your very best
and at your very worst?

I Pray This Finds You

*I can still feel the heat from the flames that burn
deep down inside the heart and the soul of
the Good Woman.
I feel the pain and the frustrations of
your heartbroken past;
I can still hear your cries in the dark asking,
"How long will this pain last?"
In your eyes, even though you smile,
I can still see the hurt through the broken glass.
So I pray for you:
"Dear God...
All I ask is that you bring peace to her soul...
that her pillow become your shoulder when her tears
begin to flow.
Please let her know...
that she is still Beautiful...
she is still Strong and that she is not alone.
Remind her that in her is the power to endure
and the strength to carry on."*

Beautiful Butterflies

My dear Beautiful, Strong Woman...
You may not know this, but you still give me butterflies.
After all this time, can you believe
I still get butterflies when I sit down to write to you.
Some may say that makes me look weak as a man...
I disagree.
I believe our ability, as men, to be honest about
how we feel, even when it makes us feel vulnerable is,
in fact, our greatest show of true strength,
emotional confidence and conviction.
To all the Good Men who may happen to read this,
if you love her...
if you trust her...
don't be afraid to show her how you really feel.
She needs that from you.

The Mind Of A Man

What goes on inside the mind of a man?
One who has been touched by the hand
and buried beneath the sands
just to be born again.
What goes on inside the mind of a man?
One who stares at his reflection
searching for all the answers to the questions
he had never cared to ask...
One who struggles to understand the very concepts
that he had never cared to grasp.
What goes on inside the mind and the heart of a man
at that very moment when he finally
decides to change...
when he finally takes in that deep breath and decides
things will never be the same?

I Believe

Many have said that I shouldn't treat you,
the Good Woman, as if you are a precious being...
that me treating your heart as being something
precious and fragile is wrong...
like, how can I call you strong and at the same time
acknowledge your weakness.
They don't understand you.
You see, it is your very weakness that
defines your strength;
it is your ability to still believe in true love
when you have little reason to believe it exists.
My dear Beautiful, Strong Woman...
No man can ever change my opinion of you;
you will always be precious and pure in my eyes
because I believe that God would never lie to me.

The Dark Knight

Somewhere out there,
there's a Good Woman waiting for the Right Man to
come into her life and say,
"I understand that you're afraid.
And although I'm not the cause of your fears,
I still feel somewhat responsible for your pains.
You see, all my life I've searched for you, and if I could
have just gotten to you sooner, I could have
protected you from the rain;
I could have protected you from all the heartaches of
having to play the Wrong Man's games.
But I'm here now...
and you don't have to worry about guarding
your heart anymore;
You can lay that burden down.
That's my job now."

I Found You...
In Me

One of you once asked me how it is that I, as a man,
can understand the heart and soul of the Good Woman...
How?
The answer is... I really don't know.
I sit alone in a dark, quiet place and I listen to
the same melody over and over again as
I try to find your space.
You know that space where all of you go
that cannot be forgotten nor can it be erased.
You see, though you all exist within different countries,
different cultures and are from different backgrounds,
you all share something special.
You may not realize it, but your hearts are so similar
that neither race, background, nor
culture can separate you. Your connection is divine.
And that space where you all come together
somehow, someway... seems to pass through my mind.

There is something truly beautiful about watching you grow. This journey has been amazing. I feel blessed that you have allowed me to be a part of yours and I am honored that you have found it in your heart to be a part of mine.

Thank You

To My dear Beautiful, Strong Woman...
I read hundreds of your emails, direct messages,
comments, and letters each week. And although I cannot
respond to all of you, each letter that I read plants a seed
in the mind and soul of a growing man.
I am man enough to admit to you that I am not nearly
the man I am capable of being... not yet.
Whether you know it or not, you're helping me.
I thank God for you, the Good Woman, and in time...
many men around the world will thank God for you too.

Acknowledgments

This is my second book, and I am both excited and nervous at the same time about what the future has in store. With that being said, I feel blessed and thankful that God has given me a second opportunity to speak with you. You have continued to inspire me and with God's help, we will continue to change the world one heart at a time.

To all of you who follow me on my different platforms, I appreciate your continued support. Please be sure to tell a friend and leave a review at your place of purchase. You may not know it, but your reviews and testimonials inspire other Beautiful, Strong Women all over the world.

To my publisher, Black Castle Media Group, thank you for everything. To my family and friends, thank you for your love and support. To my Father... thank you for being there. I appreciate you more than you know.

Lastly, I would like to say to my mother, "I love you. There is a tenderness in your heart that no words could accurately describe. Of all the mothers God could have picked for me... I am forever thankful that he chose you to be mine." Blessings.

TM

Other titles published by
Black Castle Media Group, Inc.

Reflections Of A Man by Mr. Amari Soul
BEST SELLER

Paperback Edition: ISBN 978-0-9861647-0-5
Kindle Edition: ISBN 978-0-9861647-1-2
EPUB Edition: ISBN 978-0-9861647-2-9
Hardback Limited Edition: ISBN 978-0-9861647-3-6

The Evolution Of A Girl by L.E. Bowman

Paperback Edition: ISBN 978-1-7338546-0-3
Kindle Edition: ISBN 978-1-7338546-2-7
EPUB Edition: ISBN 978-1-7338546-1-0

CPSIA information can be obtained
at www.ICGtesting.com
Printed in the USA
BVHW072251050321
601708BV00007B/7

9 780986 164774